I0503205

5 Powerful Strategies
Of Successful Entrepreneurs

Published By: AKBG Publishing
A Turning Point Enrichment Company

Gertrude J Chapman

Table Of Contents

Introduction	4
The Power Of The Subconscious Mind	7
The Power Of Your Vision	11
The Power Of Persistence	14
The Power Of Walking In Your Authority	18
The Power Of Being Organized	21
Conclusion	29

Introduction

5 Power Strategies Of Successful Entrepreneurs was written to ignite a fire in your spirit. A fire so powerful that it will give you enough fuel to pick up your dream and run full force. Are you ready for this challenge?

Cease from caring about the negative things that people have told you in the past. You may have had an inner conversation that was against your beliefs, or felt like you were born on the wrong side of the tracks. Stop entertaining those thoughts, because you have an opportunity to change.

Make a firm decision in your heart that you are sick and tired of what you are doing and the results you are seeing.

There is better out there for you. Your present situation has grown uncomfortable. Today is *Your Turning Point*.

Move out of your comfort zone. This is a place where struggling cease to exist. There are treasures all around you. Take time to enjoy your journey and what has made itself available to you.

Dedication

I dedicate this book to my immediate family, friends, fans, supporters and everyone who has given me an opportunity to speak encouragement into their lives.

5 Power Strategies Of Successful Entrepreneurs

CHAPTER 1

THE POWER OF THE

SUBCONSCIOUS MIND

The question that is often asked, "Why can I not seem to get my breakthrough?" These words have been uttered by countless individuals who are going through a series of adjustments. Yet, they are still finding themselves in the same circumstances, because of disappointment after disappointment. Thoughts about manifesting their desires become pushed farther away.

People are making outward efforts to change what they are currently facing, but at the end of the week are finding themselves exhausted. The whole idea of change becomes overwhelming and before long that person settles back into the place they were trying to escape.

Sometimes a person is expecting everything to suddenly transform and when it does not happen quickly they give up thinking maybe this is their lot in life. Settling for something and seeing their effort of trying as a failure without looking intently beyond the situation.

Change is not a superficial action, but something that has to be implemented on the inside of a person. Deep within the mind is where life altering transformations take place. The subconscious mind is the center of your thinking. Whatever thoughts that reside in your heart is your true self.

Storage of information is housed in the memory which triggers different emotions. The subconscious mind is aware of what is actually taking place, before someone engages themselves. It is unlimited at what it can do and can be transformed from limiting beliefs and habits.

Everyone has constant conversations within themselves on a daily basis. Inner conversations are constantly happening and will frame your day. Thinking on thoughts that are contrary to what is intended will sabotage a good intention. Allowing thoughts to "run through" the mind is not a wise choice.

The power of the subconscious mind is often overlooked and not given much thought. The subconscious mind is the seat of power and the mind can manifest the most dominant thoughts. Pay special attention to thoughts and carefully choose those that bring edification to positive desires.

Cease from allowing your subconscious mind to destroy your dreams, by using four ways to stop it now.

1.)   Decide from your heart that you will take a certain path toward fulfilling your goal. List your plan of action clearly and in detail. Do not make empty promises that you know you are unable to complete. Break down your goals into manageable segments, so you are able to complete each one fully. This build integrity, because your subconscious mind is storing everything. You do not want to be listed as one that waivers.

2.)   Believe that you deserve what you desire. See yourself as a worthy recipient of whatever you set your goal toward. There is nothing impossible to you, if you just believe you deserve what you are aiming for and maintain a positive and grateful attitude.

3.)   Visualize in detail and allow your five senses to participate in this exercise. See yourself physically moving in your dream. Use your hands and legs and feel the energy as you visualize walking throughout this experience. Picture yourself living your dream and your physical body will respond with the sound of increased heartbeats.

4.)   Begin doing things that are in accordance with your dream. Physically do whatever you believe to manifest. Physical actions and the above visualization technique will help bring your future into the now.

The subconscious mind is a great tool, if you know how to use it to reprogram your thoughts and live your life as it was meant to be. Train your mind to manifest the good that you wish to contribute to the world.

Everyone has something unique that is able to make a life-changing impact around the globe. Find yours, as you use the power of the subconscious mind to rise above present circumstances.

CHAPTER 2

THE POWER OF YOUR VISION

Vision is what keeps a person alive, otherwise, they are just walking around going through the motions. This course of living is just like a robot following a certain command. You have heard people say, "I am just going with the flow." What if the flow is leading them away from their desires? Have you ever found yourself in a position where you have lost your focus and all hope seems to have vanished?

This is what occurs when distractions come and you take your eyes off of your goals and begin listening to the voice of distractions. Distractions have a voice and if you are not careful it can lead you down a path and dictate terms to you. As humans, we must recognize that we have power and authority in our minds that can give life to or render a situation lifeless.

Reprogram your subconscious mind, by replacing negative and self-defeating beliefs with truth that there are no limitations in the world. Allow yourself to step outside of limitations into a world of abundance. By doing this you will begin to draw abundance to yourself. Visualize yourself surrounded by abundance.

Everyday make a conscious effort to stay on track, by keeping your visualizations fresh and positive. No matter what stage you are in life do not be content, but strive for greatness. Cease worrying how something is going to work, instead begin calling forth what you want to happen.

Visualization is seeing yourself operating in a particular capacity. Change comes with making a definite decision concerning who you want to be, what you want to do and what you want to have in life. This is creative dreaming or calling forth things into existence. You have to line up with your vision.

When desiring things to be different positive visualization will help you to reach your goals. Visualization happens all the time, so make sure that your visualization is only positive toward the things that you desire.

It is time to take your visualization into manifestation, so do not cut yourself short. Tell yourself you deserve whatever you desire. Occupy your vision. See yourself with everything that you visualize that you want to be, to do and to have in your life.

Whatever vision you occupy will come true, so be positive and definite in your visualization. Walk and move in your vision. Do not sit there on the sidelines, but get involved. Have a total experience in your mind. Feel the joy within yourself. Use your emotions when you are asking yourself these questions: "How does it feel to be___?" "How does it feel to have__?" "How does it feel to do __?"

Placing yourself in the picture makes it real and seals the vision bringing your vision into reality. Live powerful in your vision, by using all five senses. If you desire to travel to Europe, see yourself walking down the picturesque streets, feel the stones on the exterior of the buildings, hear the voices of the locals at the market, smell the aroma of the pastries and taste the freshness of the specialty dishes of the locale.

Once you begin visualizing, you will be led to do certain things in which you should comply. New ideas and resources will come your way and you should engage yourself in doing them. Things will be available to you that will lead you toward your goal.

Visualization is powerful, because it creates a picture of what you want and expect; so be careful and definite. Remember, if you cannot see yourself out of a certain situation, you will remain in that situation. So, use everything that you have to get to where you desire to go, by being definite and positive concerning your goals.

CHAPTER 3

THE POWER OF PERSISTENCE

Persistence will carry you forth, even during the times you do not feel like moving forward. Have you ever experienced those days when you just do not feel like doing anything? Especially on Monday morning, after you had a wonderful weekend with family and friends. Now you are sitting at your desk trying to get your morning started.

To you it seems like everything just remains the same no matter what you are doing. There is not any progress, instead you find yourself going through the motions of a routine.

You start thinking how to break out of this arena. Whatever you try to do there seems to be no moving forward, or even growth. Press into being persistent no matter how you are feeling right now. Allow persistence to become a motivating factor in your life.

Adopting persistence helps you to no longer depend on old ideas and ways. Instead, you begin to birth positive effective ideas that bring about life and longevity. This is especially important in the early stages, as you are just developing your business. You have to keep pressing, because there are a million negative mind triggers that will make you want to quit.

You may replay conversations you had with others. People voicing their opinion, but not understanding your vision. That is why you have to keep some things to yourself and not tell everybody everything. They will not understand your vision as you do.

Refer back to your journal where you wrote down your vision with the goals and allow yourself to be refreshed. Encourage yourself. Have a heart to heart conversation with yourself. Strengthen yourself, by adopting being persistent no matter what.

Persistence is a great way to develop confidence, because you are now seeing things in a whole different prospective. Make a choice to continue moving beyond those boundaries and be determined to reach your goals to completion.

Being persistent in business is a gateway to cultivating a future for many things in life. No one said that it was going to be easy, but you have to continue to work on your vision, if you want to succeed. Keep yourself focused on your vision, by rehearsing it over and over in your mind. No matter what it looks like now, it is only temporary.

Set a steady pace and stay on track. Refrain from making quick changes every time you are faced with opposition, instead weigh it out and get to the root of the situation.

Businesses experience interference often and you have to readily tell the difference between an outside interference and a change in business flow. Truly get to understand the ins and outs of every aspect of your business. Face those things that need to be solved and dismiss those things that are futile.

Remember, you, as the visionary, have to make it work and set the momentum in which everything flows. Charge your spirit and electrify your surroundings, so the momentum brings life within the environment.

Things are not always what they appear to be, because it depends on your attitude. The mind and eyes will play tricks on you, so avoid making changes when you are tired.

Diligently work toward finishing a project. There are many things that will unfold that will bring about a challenge. Persist though the steps and at all cost.

Challenges are good, because they sharpen you revealing abilities that you never thought you possessed. The pressure of being challenged leads you beyond your natural abilities. You enter a zone of believing you can accomplish whatever you are facing and succeed.

Allow yourself to go beyond the limits that you, for whatever reason, have set for yourself. You can do anything that you set your mind to accomplish. So, what is holding you back? Use pressure and persistence to move you beyond your comfort zone.

Persisting through the pressure has a way of removing you from all things that you have in the past used as a crutch. You only allowed yourself to go so far. Instead of facing your challenges you relied on that crutch to take the weight off.

How many times people give up, because they have been going through obstacle after obstacle and everything seems to remain the same. If that is happening to you, I challenge you to look again. Take another look at whatever you are facing and carefully design a solution to overcome those objectives.

Concealed within that objective you will be able to find keys that will not only accomplish the present opportunity, but also future ideas that you would have never thought of doing. Inside of every obstacle is a brilliant key capable of causing your business to flourish. Hiding from obstacles is not the thing to do, instead use them as stepping stones to your next area of victory.

CHAPTER 4

THE POWER OF WALKING

IN YOUR AUTHORITY

Fear is a powerful force that can render you lifeless, by causing you to miss your meeting with the components of your dream. There are a couple of things that can conquer fear. One is love, having a burning passion for what you do and the other is facing your fear head-on.

Love subdues all. Having a burning passion is able to extinguish any doubts and fears, as long as you remain focused on your goal. Know what you do and be able to explain in detail your dream. If there is any apprehension, then there is a lack of clarity and your dream is subject to attack.

Possess clarity of who you are and what you do. Clarity has the ability to keep the door closed to fear. Become acquainted with your dream in such a way that people see you and your dream as one.

Are you allowing circumstances to dictate your life? Do you know the power that you possess to render anything that presents itself before you helpless, or lifeless?

Do not take a backseat to disturbing letters, phone calls, messengers, or anything else that comes to rob you of your peace. You are the head and not the tail; you are above only and not beneath.

It may not look like it in the natural, but you are an overcomer. Victory is yours. Circumstances have to bow at your feet. Do not sit there waiting for bad news to arrive and allow it to kill your dream. Begin speaking to whatever it is now and let it know your terms.

You can create your own outcome. As a creator, design the life you wish to live and let distractions know you intend to crush them beneath your feet. Try it and see a turnaround.

It may seem that things are taking too long to get completed or solved. Be patient, because all things are working for your good. Continue to move ahead and relax, because the tide is getting ready to turn.

Let go of your fear, by facing your fear and do not give it an opportunity to paralyze and stop you from going forward. Deal with fear right away.

When you decide enough is enough and fear will no longer be a factor in your situation it loses its power and releases the grip it once had over your life.

Do what you are afraid of, like making that phone call, speaking in front of a large audience, or meeting new people. You will be astonished at the results and feel more peace in your life.

CHAPTER 5

THE POWER OF BEING ORGANIZED

Are you one who is always dreaming, but never accomplishing anything? Your dreams are excellent, but somehow you just cannot seem to get it together. You want to, but you give up, before you ever get started. Maybe you are that person who has a list of unfulfilled goals. You start, but you never complete one project.

You may be that person who jumps around from one thing to another. You heard of this idea, so you went there. You were not happy, so you heard of something else. Now you got on that bandwagon. Seeking and searching, but never coming into the reality of organizing yourself.

Everything is scattered. You see one thing. You believe another thing. Yet, you live your life still another way and never coming into the realization that within yourself nothing is working in unity. You are your vision. You are your business. When people see you they see your business.

Disorganization is one of the fastest ways to kill momentum. Years ago, I was asked to participate at this speaking event. It was a three day event and I was going to even volunteer my team, to give the event hosts some added support and publicity.

Each participant was asked for their input and if they had anyone on their team who would like to volunteer for this event. After the first meeting and several phone conversations, I came to the conclusion that I would not risk my team to this level of disorganization. I did what I could to personally get the word out, but that was as far as I would go, because I knew how to enter into this without picking up any residue.

Yes, I still kept my commitment to a point, but I refused to become involved any further. The reason being, the hosts, no matter what had been agreed upon between them and the participants, in which I was one of the participants, was doing it their way.

Teamwork, regardless of what was mentioned and asked for, was not their intent. So, I just did what I was initially asked to do. A few other things I was asked to do at the last moment and I mean just a few minutes, before I was to do it. Nothing planned, but with the hosts just winging it. I accepted, but I would have loved to show them ways to make their event successful. My business is to show people how to be successful in every area of their life.

A lot of money was spent on this event and the hosts were left deep in the red. So sad, but you cannot help anyone who refuses to be helped.

Have you ever experienced sitting down at your desk on any given day knowing that you have numerous things that you have to do and you just sit? You are inundated with tasks not only for that day, but your week is filled with things that have to be done.

Knowing you have these things, but still you remain sitting, or stumbling around the internet. As you are sitting, you notice you have nothing completed and an hour or more has passed.

What have you accomplished? When you are in a solitary moment you are picturing all the things that you have to get done and the strategy you will use to accomplish it, but now here you are just sitting. You do not know where to start, then you are too scattered to work on that project and once again you put it off for another day.

You keep pushing things further and further down the line. What may be relevant for today may not be necessary in the future. You have just missed a grand opportunity. You have allowed your time and season to expire. How many times have you tried to accomplish something and there was no longer any opportunity left for that idea?

Wasted time is money. This idle time is something that can happen to any of us when we do not properly prepare ourselves. You will begin to move off course and become distracted with things that will eat up the times when you should be producing.

Take some time and carefully plan out your goals for the current week. There are a variety of ways you can plan, track and set goals. Use a calendar. A desk calendar, calendar on a smart phone, a laptop, or a tablet. Many of the electronics can even set a reminder to alert you when one task ends and the next begins.

Do not forget to make time for a couple of breaks and lunch. Balance out your life, so it does not become cumbersome. As a business owner, it is important that you enjoy what you are doing. Take time out to make your day flow, instead of constantly fighting to catch up and finish some project.

Jot a few things down that you plan to do each day and work toward getting those responsibilities completed. Depending on your business, maybe two or three tasks per day are the max. Keep it short, because you want to flow.

Avoid trying to get everything done in one day. You have to make plans for the unexpected. If you are unable to complete a task make that the first task that you begin the next day. Allow yourself ample room for making adjustments.

On day two, you may have to move one task that you planned to day three, but that is okay. Likewise, there may be some time left over, before the end of the day where you can get started early on a task for the upcoming day.

Make every moment productive, as you strive to stay on course and complete that task. The mistake comes when people set unrealistic goals and become overwhelmed, because nothing gets done and they just give up and start freestyling.

You have to have a plan, because freestyling causes you to become involved with other things that distracts you from accomplishing your goals.

Does that sound familiar? Well, if it does acknowledge it and fix those things and get back on track. Being organized helps you to be productive each day.

You will be energized to make positive changes and embrace looking forward to reaching your goals at the end of the week. Monday mornings will be welcomed, because your mind will be clear.

A major time waster that leads to being disorganized is having a scattered mind. There are pieces of the project all over the place, and before one task is completed, another task has begun.

This is a real issue here. Many people out there are well-meaning, but they just somehow cannot put those tasks together to complete a project. These are starters, but not finishers.

Their minds are constantly racing ahead, but sitting down and planning is not one of their attributes. If this describes you, find someone who has the characteristic of being a finisher and allow them to work to see the project through to completion.

Teamwork is so vital in business and should never be overlooked. Some people fail to see themselves standing in the position where their genius will come alive, because they are trying to do it all. Hire others who are strong in those areas of your weaknesses.

Successful business owners hire people who are smarter than they are and have the skills that are greater than theirs. Maintain the position where you are flourishing and allow others to blossom in their strengths.

Strive for your business to be organized in every area of operation, from the visionary to the receptionist and everyone in between.

Set a pattern for all employees to follow, because when you are working in an organized business it is quicker to catch mistakes and avoid unnecessary delays. Mistakes will happen and other things may also arise, but you will be able to pinpoint errors and business slumps sooner.

Being organized is structure on which you can build and it provides a solid foundation for everything that will be built on top of it.

Organization shapes the frame of the business avoiding a sudden collapse and allows room for growth. Growth is a positive factor, so it is wise to make a decision to bring everything into an alignment, by adapting yourself to have an organized business life.

You only have one life, so make the best of what you possess and enjoy your life to the fullest. Make a decision to begin right where you are to alleviate any unnecessary stress that you have, because of the added pressure of being disorganized.

CONCLUSION

You are designed for greatness to not only change your life, but being a life-changer to someone else. You are a great man or woman of destiny. No one can do it like you can get it done.

Here is your opportunity to step out and let your gifts, talents and abilities shine. Hope you are enlightened and inspired to implement these 5 power strategies into your life.

As always, *"This Is Your Time. This Is Your Season. This Is YOUR TURNING POINT!"* ™

NOTES

NOTES

ABOUT THE AUTHOR

Executive Producer & Radio Host of Your Turning Point Motivational Mondays on BlogTalk Radio.

Founder/President & CEO of Turning Point

Enrichment, Inc.

Author of 6 Books on Amazon.com

Wrote and Self- Published 6 Motivational Books that were distributed to conference attendees.

A regular Contributor to E-zine Articles.

Conducts Quarterly Empowerment Webinars.

A Speaker in Empowerment Conferences and Entrepreneur Seminars.

The Author of 3 E-Booklets to Supercharge Your Life.

The Editor and Founder of AKBG Publishing.

The Author, Narrator and Producer of the Media Training Audio Program "Your Turning Point."

Minister Of The Gospel, Wife, Mother and Grandmother.

BOOKING FOR SPEAKING ENGAGEMENTS

Gertrude J Chapman

Turning Point Enrichment, Inc.

www.turningpointenrichment.com

turningpointenrichment@gmail.com

(407) 668-6828

SOCIAL MEDIA

Facebook.com

https://www.facebook.com/TurningPointEnrichment

Twitter.com

https://twitter.com/pastorgertrude

https://twitter.com/gertrudechapman

Linkedin.com

https://www.linkedin.com/in/gertrudechapman

Pinterest.com

https://www.pinterest.com/gertrudechapman/

Facebook

http://facebook.com/turningpointenrichmentinternationalministries

E-zine

http://ezinearticles.com/?expert=Gertrude_Chapman

BlogTalk Radio

http://blogtalkradio.com/your-turning-point

BOOKS ON AMAZON

Not Willing That Any Should Perish: Do You Really Love People The Way That Jesus Loves People

ISBN #1515210820

40 Days Of Motivation For The Soul

ISBN #1515091791

10 Keys To Succeeding In Business For The Entrepreneur

ISBN #151488853x

The Year Of The Lord's Release

ISBN #1506187641

Motivation From Within Leveraging Your Power

ISBN #1451519702

Esther A Woman Chosen For Her Generation: Unlocking The Keys To Kingdom Living

ISBN #1507754310

5 Power Strategies Of Successful Entrepreneurs

5 Power Strategies Of Successful Entrepreneurs

5 Power Strategies Of Successful Entrepreneurs

www.ingramcontent.com/pod-product-compliance
Lightning Source LLC
Chambersburg PA
CBHW071020180526
45168CB00003B/1495